HANDWRITING FOR
MINECRAFTERS

Cursive

Illustrated by Amanda Brack

Sky Pony Press
New York

Copyright © 2018 by Hollan Publishing, Inc.

Minecraft® is a registered trademark of Notch Development AB.

The Minecraft game is copyright © Mojang AB.

Sky Pony Press books may be purchased in bulk at special discounts for sales promotion, corporate gifts, fund-raising, or educational purposes. Special editions can also be created to specifications. For details, contact the Special Sales Department, Sky Pony Press, 307 West 36th Street, 11th Floor, New York, NY 10018 or info@skyhorsepublishing.com.

Sky Pony® is a registered trademark of Skyhorse Publishing, Inc.®, a Delaware corporation.

Minecraft® is a registered trademark of Notch Development AB.
The Minecraft game is copyright © Mojang AB.

Visit our website at www.skyponypress.com.

10 9 8 7 6 5 4

Library of Congress Cataloging-in-Publication Data is available on file.

Cover art by Bill Greenhead

Cover design by Brian Peterson

Interior art by Amanda Brack

Book design by Kevin Baier

Print ISBN: 978-1-5107-3254-4

Printed in China

A NOTE TO PARENTS

Parents know just as well as teachers that adding fun to schoolwork helps to motivate kids and enhance their learning.

Handwriting for Minecrafters: Cursive is the ultimate in kid-friendly handwriting practice. With their favorite game characters to guide them through the alphabet, kids will be eager to master cursive letter formation. All it takes is one page of guided practice a day to reinforce what kids are learning in the classroom and encourage continued academic success.

Added features like numbered strokes and traceable practice rows keep frustration to a minimum, build confidence, and help kids learn correct cursive letter formation one step at a time.

Kids who master the alphabet can move on to more advanced practice including writing their name, copying complete sentences, and crafting their own creative Minecrafting sentences.

Whether it's the joy of seeing their favorite game characters on every page or the thrill of seeing the progress they're making, this workbook is designed to entice even the most reluctant student.

Happy adventuring!

a *Apple*

a *a a a a*

a apple

1 *a* 2 3 *a* *a* *a* *a*

B

Blaze

1 2 3 4

b   *blaze*

b   *b*   *b*   *b*   *b*

C

Creeper

C C C C C C

c   creeper

1 2 *c*   *c*   *c*   *c*   *c*

D   *Diamonds*

d  diamonds

d

1 d 3
2

Ender dragon

e

ender dragon

1 *e* 2   *e*   *e*   *e*   *e*

F

Fishing rod

f

fishing rod

f   *f*   *f*   *f*   *f*

G   Guardian

g   *guardian*

1 2 3 *g*   *g*   *g*   *g*   *g*

H *Husk*

h

husk

h   h   h   h   h   h

I   *Iron golem*

i

iron golem

i *i* *i* *i* *i*

$\mathcal{J}$

$\mathcal{Jockey}$

$\mathcal{J}$

$\mathcal{J}$ $\mathcal{J}$ $\mathcal{J}$ $\mathcal{J}$

j

jockey

j   1→ ↓2   *j*   *j*   *j*   *j*
     3↺
4

K

Killer bunny

K K K K K

k  *killer bunny*

1 2 3 4

k   k   k   k

L Lapis lazuli

L L L L L L

l

lapis lazuli

l

M Mooshroom

m m m m m m

$\mathcal{m}$  $\mathcal{mooshroom}$

$\mathcal{m}$

1 2 3

$\mathcal{m} \quad \mathcal{m} \quad \mathcal{m} \quad \mathcal{m}$

n

Nether wart

n n n n n

N

nether wart

1 $\mathcal{N}$ 2 $\mathcal{N}$ $\mathcal{N}$ $\mathcal{N}$ $\mathcal{N}$

O *Ocelot*

ocelot

$\mathcal{P}$

Portal

_p_

portal

$\mathcal{Q}$ Quartz

$\mathcal{Q}$

q

quartz

q   q   q   q   q

R

Resources

resources

S Slime

2
3
1
S S S S S

s   *slime*

1 2
s   *s*   *s*   *s*   *s*
3

T.N.T.

t

t. n. t.

1 2 3 *t*   *t*   *t*   *t*   *t*

43

$\mathcal{U}$ Upside down

$\mathcal{U}$ $\mathcal{U}$ $\mathcal{U}$ $\mathcal{U}$ $\mathcal{U}$

𝓊𝓊 *upside down*

𝓊𝓊

V

Villager

$\mathcal{U}$ villager

$\mathcal{U}$ $\mathcal{U}$ $\mathcal{U}$ $\mathcal{U}$ $\mathcal{U}$

1 2 3

$\mathcal{W}$

$\mathcal{W}olf$

$\mathcal{W}$ $\mathcal{W}$ $\mathcal{W}$ $\mathcal{W}$ $\mathcal{W}$

w

wolf

1 2 3 4 *w* *w* *w* *w* *w*

X-ray mod

x  x-ray mod

x

$\mathcal{Y}$

$\mathcal{Y}ellow$

$\mathcal{Y}$ $\mathcal{Y}$ $\mathcal{Y}$ $\mathcal{Y}$ $\mathcal{Y}$

y   yellow

1 2 3 y   y   y   y   y

Z

Zombie

pigman

zombie

pigman

Z

REVIEW THE ALPHABET

Practice the whole alphabet below!

NAME PRACTICE

Practice writing your name on the lines below and at right.

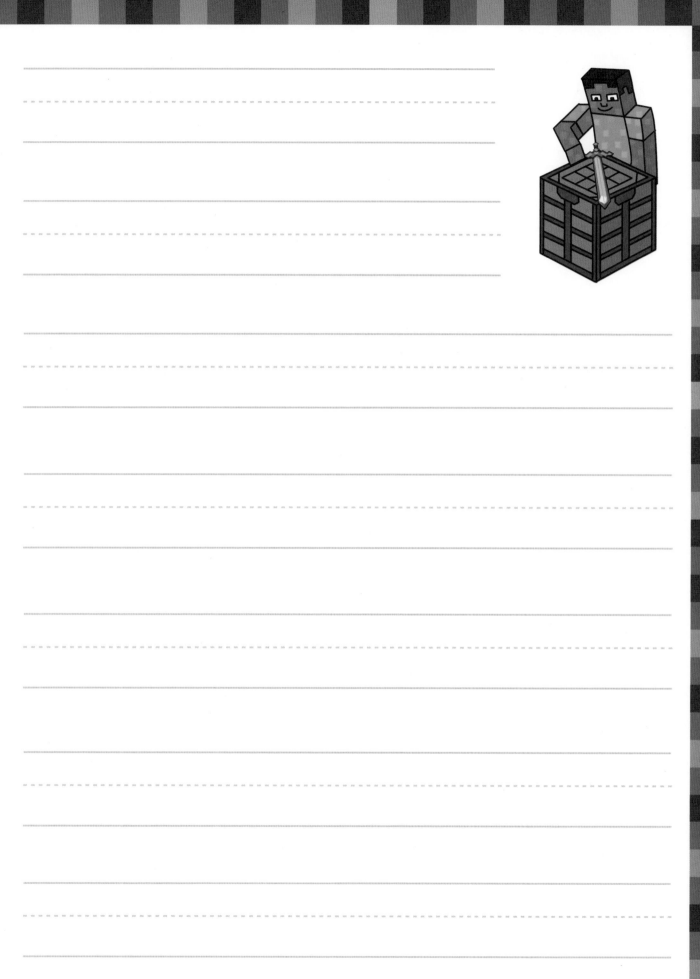

SENTENCE PRACTICE

Copy each sentence on the line below.

 Try to build a

shelter by nightfall.

 If you don't, a

zombie will get you.

Chop trees to

get wood for a shelter.

You'll need a

torch when it's dark.

Watch out for spiders!

Zombies burn

up in the daylight.

Skeletons shoot

their arrows at you.

Throw a splash potion!

Explore the

Nether if you dare.

Find the treasure

chest filled with emeralds

and diamonds.

CRAFT YOUR OWN

Write your own Minecrafting sentences (or a story!) below in cursive and share it with a friend or parent.